Made Only
FOR Heaven

Learning to praise through the
pain of miscarriage and
stillbirth

WENDY CARR

Made Only For Heaven
Learning to praise through the pain of miscarriage and stillbirth
by Wendy Carr

Printed in the United States of America.

ISBN 9781498454148

Scripture quotations taken from the King James Version (KJV)
– *public domain*

Cover Design: Shannon Gaines

www.xulonpress.com

Reviews

I do not know a woman who wouldn't profit from reading this book! Wendy has an openness about her strengths and weaknesses through these trials that is heart gripping. For those who have never experienced the devastation of losing a child, you will walk away from this book better equipped to understand and comfort those who have experienced this type of loss.

~ Charity Teis Berkey, Pastors wife in Las Vegas, NV

There have been few books written on the topic of miscarriage, but even less written about loss through the middle of a pregnancy. Having experienced such a loss at 22 weeks of pregnancy, this book would have been a tremendous encouragement. Made Only For Heaven will be an excellent tool to minister to families who suffer from this type of loss.

~ Jennifer Baker, Pastors wife in French Lick, IN

In both of my miscarriages, I will never forget the moments when I realized that something was wrong. You just don't think it will ever happen to you. I wish I had known all the heartache and physical pain of a miscarriage earlier in my life so I could have been a better support to others who were going through this journey. Made Only for Heaven will not only be a great tool to help women know they are not alone in the emotions and hurt they feel during this time— but will also provide solace and comfort in embracing the fact that each baby is with their creator who loves them more than we ever could.

~ Shannon Gaines, wife, mother, and graphic designer

Dedication

To my wonderful husband, the man who faithfully walks by my side through our journey of life. I love you, more.

Acknowledgements

*T*his book could not have been put together without the Lord and all glory belongs to Him. Without Him I would not have made it through all of these losses and I give thanks to Him for His steadfast love and faithfulness. This book is a direct result of answered prayer and I will forever be grateful to Him for the healing He has brought to my heart.

To my husband Chad, the one who has stood by my side, loved me unconditionally, and continually makes me feel like the most cherished woman. Thank you for your encouragement through it all and especially your support in writing this book. I could not have done it without you. I love you!

To my family and friends, thank you for your encouragement and support through joyful times and through our darkest valleys. Your prayers and encouragement are deeply appreciated and helped make this book possible. Thank you for your encouragement, assistance, and guidance as I worked to complete this book.

To Bethlie Young, thank you for all of your encouragement along the way. You are a dear friend and I am deeply thankful for you and that the Lord allowed our paths to cross several years ago. What a gem you are!

To my editors and designer, thank you for your countless hours of work to see this book to completion. I could not have done it without you.

And finally, thank you-the reader. My heart's prayer is that you will be encouraged and truly find healing in Christ alone.

Contents

Forward

" O taste and see that the LORD is good: blessed is the man that trusteth in Him." (Psalm 34:8) Does this seem to be an odd verse to share at the beginning of a book about miscarriage and infant loss? How can we, who have been through such bitter heartache, still taste of the goodness of our God? I can tell you, because I've been there, it is a journey. It is a journey of sorrow, pain, fear, and doubt. It is a journey that will leave you tasting only the bitterness of life...or tasting the better goodness of God.

Wendy Carr has been on this journey. I was honored to meet Pastor Chad Carr and his lovely wife Wendy shortly after the birth of their stillborn son. Even then, as she was struggling with the extreme pain of such a loss, she had a sweet, yet determined, spirit to seek the Lord. In the years since, we have kept in touch, and I am always encouraged and blessed by her willingness to see the goodness of God in sunshine or storm.

Not only has Wendy come through the loss of her little ones knowing and loving God more, she has been burdened to share her journey with other hurting mothers... ladies who may feel desolately alone in their grief. In her book, Made Only for Heaven, Wendy shares her heartache, and at times, the raw emotion, that accompanied each loss. But she doesn't stop with the sorrow and pain; she also shares the healing that comes through trusting the Lord in the midst of the sorrow and pain. She will share with you the peace that comes from truly tasting and knowing that the Lord is good.

Sincerely,
Bethlie Young
Wife of Evangelist David Young

Chapter One

This Is Not Your Fault

*L*earning to praise God through life's trials can sometimes be nothing short of difficult! Praising the Lord can be quite challenging when He allows trials in our lives. They are not something we enjoy, yet they are certainly needful. Most often during our hard times, we have the opportunity to learn much more about our great and loving God! When our faith is stretched, we can be confident that the Lord is close by and will not abandon us in our time of need.

Choosing to praise the Lord through life's trials is a choice God's children have to make. We are all faced with the decision to either allow God to use our difficulties to help refine us and draw us ever closer to His side or to turn the opposite direction and run from His loving arms. Philippians 4:4 admonishes us,

"Rejoice in the Lord alway: and again I say, Rejoice."

For those that grew up in a Christian home, this verse was probably one of the first Bible verses learned as a child. Although an easy verse to learn, rejoicing in the Lord always is not always easy. We have our own plans and dreams for our lives, and trials never seem to fit into the plans we make.

Even though we may try to deny it, most of us desire a fairytale life. This desire starts from the time we are children. As little girls, we enjoyed dressing up in fancy dresses. As we looked into the mirror, our imaginations would run wild. We saw a beautiful princess in need of a prince!

As we grew up, those fancy dresses were packed away because we were too old to play with such childish things. Instead, we began teasing our hair and searching for just the right outfit in order to catch the eye of that one particular boy. Before we knew it, high school came and went. As we waved good-bye to our friends and said hello to college life, the dream to find Prince Charming was in the forefront of many young girls' minds.

When I was sixteen, I remember having a conversation with my mom about how I only wanted to date the guy I was going to marry. I had read an article about a young girl around my age beginning a journal to her future husband and thought it was a great idea and began one of my own! I wrote him letters and included a prayer for him at the end of each entry. Whenever I thought about him, whoever he was, I pulled out that journal and wrote some more. Though I had a few dates at college, I just had not met "Mr. Right". When I would complain to my mom about the many dateless nights I had, she would remind me of the conversation we had when I was in high school. Instead of dating around, I made some great girlfriends, and we did most everything together! I also kept adding entries into the journal I had started for my future husband along with praying fervently for him, whoever he was.

I met my Prince Charming my senior year of college. Chad called me up one day out of the blue and asked me to meet him for dinner. Though I tried with all my heart to play it cool, my heart was pounding so hard I was certain he could hear it through the phone. Throughout the course of the next year and a half, we became the best of friends. Our love for each other grew immensely and we spent hours together talking, praying, and dreaming of our future together. As we grew closer in our relationship to Christ, we began to grow closer together in our relationship. As time went on, the Lord made it evident to us that we were meant to spend the rest of our lives together. I remember calling my mom and informing her that this man was "the one" for me. There was such a peace in my heart. I was certain that he was the one for me, for as long as we both shall live.

That day finally came. On June 4th of 2005, I vowed my life, my heart, my all to the man of my dreams as he did to me. It did not matter what the future held. The only thing that mattered was the fact that we were in love and we were thrilled to finally be married! The weather was perfect. Our wedding was held in northern California at my home church. Usually in June, the weather is rather hot. Not that day. It was in the 70's, and a slight breeze was blowing. It was absolutely perfect. That day was the best day of my life! The Lord saw fit to bless me with a husband who loved the Lord and me with all of his heart and I will forever be thankful to the Lord for blessing me with my sweet and wonderful husband!

After a beautiful wedding and honeymoon in the Upper Peninsula of Michigan, we began to settle into our newly found life together. We began our daily routines, and before we knew it, the summer had slipped right by. I was starting my first year of teaching while my husband worked in construction coupled with being a part time youth pastor. Life was great. So in love with each other and the life the Lord had given us. Just as in the fairytales, we were living our happily ever after!

In November of 2005, we discovered we were expecting our very first baby. A precious gift from the Lord who represented the love Chad and I had for each other. We were overflowing with excitement! We had the first prenatal appointment. Everything seemed to be right on track, so we informed our parents about our coming baby. They were thrilled to be getting a new grandbaby added to the family. Life really seemed to be perfect.

The morning after my appointment, I woke up early as usual to get ready for my day of teaching. When I climbed out of bed, I experienced some rather sharp pain all across my abdomen. I tried to carry on with getting ready for work and shake it off, but I failed miserably. I woke up my husband and explained the pain I had been experiencing. It was near impossible to stand, sit, or even lay down without intense pain being present. After little debate, we headed to the ER. We called some family members on our way and gave them a few details along with a request for prayer. The wait in the ER was not terribly long. I remember that the news broadcast of the morning was echoing in the silent waiting, room while a man in the corner was attempting to get a coke out of a nearby vending machine. I remember sitting in that room afraid of the unknown. Afraid for my new baby and wondering what could be wrong.

A nurse eventually came out, and we were taken back to our own private room. The nurse took a few blood samples and started an IV. As she left the room, she threw instructions over her shoulder to put on the less than attractive hospital gown she left sitting on the bed. A few minutes later, the doctor came in and told us he was going to order some ultrasounds to be done since I was expecting. How exciting! We would get to see our baby for the first time! After a few ultrasounds, we discovered the following three things: number one, I was actually eight weeks along; number two, the baby had no heartbeat; and number three, I was in need of emergency surgery because the baby was actually in my fallopian tube. What?! I was only coming in to find a simple answer about the pains I was having, now I'm expected to have surgery? The news completely threw us off guard. As I was wheeled back into my ER room, I began sobbing. The thought of surgery frightened me. The grief of knowing my baby had not survived was rather overwhelming, especially for 6:30 in the morning. Because we had already seen the baby had no heartbeat, we went ahead and scheduled the surgery right away.

My heart was terrified. Not only had I never undergone surgery before, but I felt a tremendous amount of guilt for my baby not surviving the pregnancy. I was checked into a hospital room to wait out my time before surgery. Our pastor came in and brought with him encouraging passages of Scripture such as 2 Timothy 1:7 which states:

"For God hath not given us the spirit of fear; but of power, and of love, and of a sound mind."

21

Even though I was facing surgery, the Lord was fully capable of giving me a peaceful heart and a sound mind if I would only let Him. The time finally came for me to be wheeled away to surgery. I said my tearful good-bye to my new husband, and off I went. My groom stepped into the waiting room and watched his new bride be wheeled away. It wasn't until later that I found out he completely broke down as he waited for me, his wife to come out of surgery. He was fearful of losing his new bride. As I lay on the hospital gurney outside the operating room, what seemed like a hundred thoughts raced through my mind at the same time. The anesthesiologist came over to me and explained what they were going to do. He picked up my freezing hand and with compassion in his eyes said, "This is not your fault. I know you are blaming yourself for what has happened, but this is not your fault. Sometimes it just happens." His words were so kind and exactly what I needed to hear as the tears I tried so hard to hold back began to trickle down.

As I climbed on the chilly operating table, my body began shaking uncontrollably. The nurses were so sweet and brought me five blankets they had in the warmer. They felt so wonderful against my cold shaking body which was in shock. I remember staring at the ceiling and observing those big lights overhead that one would see in television shows and movies. It was completely surreal. "Now begin to count to ten," the anesthesiologist instructed. I only remember reaching number two before the medicine did its job, and I was out.

Waking up in the recovery room was no easy task. My body only wanted to sleep but the stubborn nurses kept prodding me to wake up! My loving husband was waiting for me in my room when the nurses brought me back. We both cried, out of relief that the surgery was over and with grief over the loss of our child. We simply clung to each other. This was quite the trial we were dealing with. Being married only five months and already reeling in the loss of our baby was not something we expected to happen. It was not in the plans we had for our lives. The nurses informed me of the pain that I would be in and the doctor already had a prescription written for me. The physical pain could be easily treated. The emotional pain on the other hand was something else. My heart had been shattered. Dreams for that were born the moment the pregnancy test said positive, were suddenly dashed. I felt I was no longer a mother. My arms were still empty. No, there was no prescription that could heal the deep wound that was gaping open in my heart.

The doctor who performed my surgery came a little while later to see how I was doing and to explain what had just taken place in the operating room. She informed us just how close to death I had come and if we had not come in when we did, I could have very easily bled to death within a few hours. We were amazed at how the Lord had protected my life!

Late that night after some discharge instructions were given, I was released. A nurse wheeled me down to the lobby. While Chad was picking up our vehicle, she asked me if I had a certain procedure done, a procedure that most commonly is done in an abortion clinic to eliminate the growing life inside the womb. "No." I replied emphatically. "My baby died and I had to have surgery". As soon as the words left my mouth, grief completely settled in. My husband pulled up in our car, and I was helped into the front seat. There was a winter storm taking place outside and the roads were icy. As we left the hospital parking lot and made our way to the stop light we hit a patch of black ice causing our car to begin doing circles all the way through the middle of the intersection. I wanted to scream, but my physical pain kept me from making any noises louder than a squeak! The Lord had His hand on us for sure because no cars were coming as we spun out of control in the middle of the intersection. Our car suffered no damage. After getting our composure and thanking the Lord for His protection, we kept on driving toward home. Thankfully the rest of our trip was uneventful. The struggle that was to come in the months ahead was not anything I was prepared for, but the Lord had much to teach this new wife and now grieving mother.

Chapter Two

The Struggle Is Real

The week this event took place was just before Thanksgiving. I was given the next week of school off to recover both physically and emotionally. There was no way on earth I was ready to just dive back into school a few days after having surgery. During those next several days, I did some real searching of God's Word. I desired to have answers that didn't exist as to why this all happened, and more than anything, I was in desperate need of encouragement. The Lord did guide in my Bible study time and led me to verses that would help to encourage my heart and build my confidence in God.

There is a passage of Scripture that most people think of when they lose a child. It is found in 2 Samuel chapter 12, and it is about the loss of David and Bathsheba's child. David is clearly mourning for his child and calls out in verse 23,

"But now he is dead, wherefore should I fast? can I bring him back again? I shall go to him, but he shall not return to me."

Most believers use this passage of Scripture to encourage themselves that their child is in Heaven, which means he cannot come back to earth, but those who are saved will one day go to Heaven and see their child. I had read this passage of Scripture before but had never appreciated it the way I did when I read it after the loss of our baby. I found it deeply encouraging to know that one day I will see my baby in Heaven.

I also found comfort in reading the Psalms. I remember reading over and over Psalm 43:5 which says,

"Why art thou cast down, O my soul? and why art thou disquieted within me? hope in God: for I shall yet praise him, who is the health of my countenance, and my God."

Despite the trial we were going through, it was possible to truly praise God. He was and still is our hope! Also in Psalm 57:2 the Psalmist writes,

> *"I will cry unto God most high; unto God that performeth all things for me".*

The first half of the verse tells us to cry unto God! Have you ever done that, dear friend? Have you ever just poured your heart out to the only One that can hear and understand? It is so easy to turn to other people to share the deepest wounds of our hearts with. Yet, God is the One that wants to put His arms of love around us and help heal the wounds. He is most often easily forgotten because we cannot literally see Him with our eyes, but He is the One that can heal our hearts best. The second half of the verse was a great reminder that God was not doing this *to* us rather He was allowing it to happen *for* us and for our good and His glory. He is not a mean God. He is, quite honestly, just the opposite. He is a loving God, and as the Psalmist put it so beautifully in Psalm 68:19,

> *"Blessed be the Lord, who daily loadeth us with benefits, even the God of our salvation. Selah"*

Even when I do not see it or am unaware of His blessings, He still chooses to daily load me up with His blessings, just as He does in your life every day. As my husband and I prayed together daily, we asked the Lord to help us handle this trial in the right way, and the Lord began to bring about peace and healing to our hearts.

Though healing from the loss of our baby came, throughout the months that followed, I struggled with not having a baby of my own. I would often dwell on the fact that I had lost my baby. My attention was often on what the Lord took away instead of what He had already given me, not to mention the tricks my mind played on me every month. The money we spent in pregnancy tests throughout that year I am sure was enough to fund a nice vacation on a cruise line! It became something of an obsession for me, wanting a baby. I felt like I was failing my husband by not being able give him a child. Now, I must interject here and comment that my husband did not share the same opinion as me. He constantly reminded me that he was perfectly content if the Lord never saw fit to grant us children here on earth. He has always been incredibly sweet and thoughtful. However, with the age we were in life, all of our friends were beginning to grow their families one by one and with each new phone call I would receive, it made my own burden heavier.

I remember a friend informing me of how excited she and her husband were about the upcoming arrival of their baby. They were excited to be the "first" of all their friends to have a baby she said. In that instant, I knew that my baby had already been forgotten. That he did not "count" because he was not on this earth and visible to the world. Those words cut into my heart so deeply. Though my friend was unintentional in hurting me, those words stung my heart deeply as they were a strong reminder once again of the loss we had endured. There are so many mothers who have lost a baby and struggle with the fact that though their children are in Heaven, it hurts to know they seem to be forgotten by others here on earth. I tried to act like I was not affected by the hurtful words, but inside I was already in tears. It was such a hard time in life and a real valley that seemed dark and long.

As I look back on that time in our life, I still do not have the answers, and I miss my first baby something awful! It is amazing the instant love a mother can have for her baby the moment she knows he or she is in her womb! What a gift that bond is the Lord has given to mother's and babies. Yet through this trial, the Lord had so much to teach me. I was coveting something, someone really which the Lord was not ready for me to have. I was discontent with the decision the Lord had made without my consent, and He had some working to do on my heart.

It was during these months that the Lord brought me to a passage in Scripture that I had previously memorized but found it so much more applicable at that moment. In Hebrews 13:5 it simply instructs,

"Let your conversation be without covetousness; and be content with such things as ye have: for He hath said, I will never leave thee nor forsake thee."

Ouch. That verse smote my heart something fierce. I knew I was not content. I knew I was not letting my conversation be without covetousness. Sadly, I did not even care at times that I was sinning! After all, what was so wrong with *wanting* a baby? A baby is a GREAT and WONDERFUL thing to want!!

Though a baby is a wonderful addition to a family, the problem came with where my heart was. In Psalm 37:4 it says

"Delight thyself also in the Lord; and He shall give thee the desires of thine heart."

Now most of us, myself included, *really* like the last half of that verse! Giving us the desires of our hearts is something we all want and most often think we deserve! However, we can not have the last half of the verse without obeying the first part. Who was I delighting in at the time? It was certainly not the Lord. There came a time when I had a choice to make. I needed to come to a place in my life when I honestly told the Lord, "even if it is only You, Chad and me for as long as we both shall live, I will still love and serve You." I truly believe the Lord wanted me to learn to be completely content with only Him and my husband before He could add any more blessings to our life.

The Lord is really all I need and yet He had already seen fit to bless me with my wonderful husband. But, there I was wanting something more! It was not wrong to desire having a baby. It was wrong that wanting a baby became more important to me at the time than God and His perfect will for our life.

Now I would love to tell you here and now that the struggle ended there. That I got my ducks in a row and never stumbled once with being content, but I can't. Truth is, I did struggle, and as the due date of a friend of mine drew ever closer, I began to pray earnestly. I knew that I would get a phone call soon informing me of the arrival of their baby. I begged God to help me. When I answered the anticipated phone, call I wanted nothing more than to share in her excitement! I did not want to covet the gift the Lord had given her. I did not want to be jealous. I just wanted to revel in her excitement and truly be joyful for her and her family.

The day came sooner then what I thought I was ready for. The phone rang, and as I reached to pick it up, I saw who it was on my caller I.D. I looked to the Heavens and quickly said, "Help me Lord!" and cheerfully answered, "Hello?" The voice on the other end was that of my dear friend and now new mother. As she began to relay the details of her delivery that we women enjoy hearing, I realized the Lord was answering my prayer. I was not envious or jealous, rather all that was in my heart was pure contentment and joy on her behalf. You know, the Lord wants to answer our prayers! He desires to help us in our times of need, if only we would ask!

James 1:6 says,

> *"But let him ask in faith, nothing wavering. For he that wavereth is like a wave of the sea driven with the wind and tossed."*

This whole time God was just waiting for me to ask for His help and *believe* that He would answer. Sometimes asking God is the easy part, the problem comes with *believing* He will and wants to answer. This verse reminds me of another passage in Scripture in the Old Testament. In I Kings 18, we can find the story of Elijah and the prophets of Baal. Elijah is fed up with the children of Israel "riding the fence" as to who they serve. He finally informed them that it was high time to choose *this* day who they would serve. Apparently, they needed an object lesson and physical proof of who the One True God was and still is. So the altar was prepared and the prophets of Baal failed miserably at calling down fire from Heaven. No matter how much they cried out to Baal, there was nothing in return. When it was Elijah's time to offer up his sacrifice, he built up his altar properly. Because he was expecting God to answer, he not only built his altar, but he had the sacrifice, the altar and a surrounding trench filled with water. Then he prayed. This was his prayer beginning in verse 36 and ending in verse 37,

"Lord God of Abraham, Isaac, and of Israel, let it be known this day that thou art God in Israel, and that I am thy servant, and that I had done all these things at thy word. Hear me, O Lord, hear me, that this people may know that thou art the Lord God, and that thou hast turned their heart again."

Wow! This man was serious about his prayers! He prayed expecting God to answer. When I read these verses, I find no wavering, no hesitation, just a simple plea to God to answer his prayer. He prayed believing God would answer and God did! The Lord sent fire from Heaven to consume the sacrifice that Elijah had prepared. What would seem to be an impossible miracle, actually took place! God hears the prayers of His children and delights in answering them!

I have always been a firm believer that God does not give us desires in our hearts to only taunt us with them. He is not a cruel God. He does not dangle our desires in front of our faces and then pull them away just as they are within our grasp. When we are delighting ourselves in God, then He begins to fill His desires in our hearts. I believe He either answers those desires when He is ready, or He removes them completely or helps us to deal with our desire properly. The desire to have a baby was still in my heart, but I had learned to be content with where the Lord had me in life. That is when it happened. Almost an exact month after talking with my friend it happened. The Lord heard my prayer and He chose to answer the desire of my heart. I was once again pregnant!

Chapter Three

When The Lord Gave

I remember like it was yesterday when we found out we were expecting our daughter. It took us a year from the time we lost our first baby to be able to get pregnant with our little girl. As a matter of fact, the day we found out I was expecting was the exact same day only one year later from when we lost our first baby. I was suspecting I might be pregnant, but I did not want to get my hopes up only to have them be dashed. Around 6 in the morning on a Saturday, I woke up and decided "today is the day!" I took the test and watched in utter disbelief as the little blue lines showed "You are a mommy again!" The giddy excitement in me swelled to great measures. I could hardly contain my excitement!

I felt like a kid at Christmas! Like a child would run to the Christmas tree, I ran to the bedroom and woke up my husband in a hurry! I knew he would forgive me for robbing him of those few precious moments that remained for him to sleep. Not knowing what to say because of my utter excitement and disbelief, as soon as I could see his eyeballs, I shoved the test in his hand. He sat straight up in bed and looked from the test to me and back again at the test. He was just as thrilled as I was and immediately began kissing me. I have no doubt we looked like two little children filled with all of our excitement! After we calmed down a bit, we immediately got on our knees. We wanted to praise and thank the Lord for entrusting us with this new precious little life! Though we were thrilled at the thought of being parents, we also prayed for wisdom because we wanted more than anything to raise this little person for Christ. We wanted to start out being parents on the right track. One can never start to early to pray for their children!

My pregnancy was perfect. My doctor was amazing, and we developed a great relationship with her. On July 10 of the next year, and one week later then her due date mind you, our sweet little Emma was born into our family. One of the greatest loves of my life was small enough to fit in my arms. She was so sweet and completely precious. Our little girl was dramatic from the start with all the crying she did when she made her appearance! Holding our tiny newborn brought immense healing to our hearts. The Lord had heard and answered our prayers! Chad and I have loved every moment with our little girl, and we thank the Lord for gifting her to us. She if full of life and joy and has such an expressive person-ality! She loves people and in her eyes everyone is a friend waiting to happen! As we watched her grow that first year, we treasured every milestone she accomplished. From rolling over to sitting up and all the wonderful baby "firsts", it was such a joy to expe-rience it all with her! With the birth of our little girl, we learned that children truly are a heritage from the Lord. A blessing not to be taken for granted.

When our little darling was 15 months old, we discovered we were expecting once again! We had desired to grow our family again for some time but obviously the Lord is the one with the perfect timing, not us. We were just as thrilled to find out about this new miracle as we were when we were expecting little Emma! We found out via my twenty week ultrasound that this time around we were having a little boy! I was shocked, I was almost certain he was a girl! What in the world was I going to do with a boy?! I did not have a clue as to how to raise a little boy, I mean, come on, I'm a girl! My husband laughed at me when I voiced my thought's to him and he replied with, "Don't worry honey, we'll be fine".

We began shopping for little boy clothes as soon as the ultrasound was over, and I started warming up to the idea of a little man in the house. By the time my due date arrived in June, I was ready to meet this little guy! Being quite the early bird, he made his entrance into this world at 4 o'clock in the morning. As soon as I saw him, I fell in love all over again with him. A little boy all our own! Everything about him was precious. As he has grown it has been fun watching the differences between him and his sister. He is certainly one-hundred percent boy! He loves dirt, food and makes all the little boy sounds that boys are just born knowing how to make! If something has wheels on it he just KNOWS what to do with it! He has a mischievous twinkle in his eye but a smile that will light up anyone's day! Yes, this cute little guy was the perfect fit into our family.

When our little Josiah was only seven months old, we discovered that I was once again expecting. Surprise! We were completely taken off guard by this one, but thrilled nonetheless. The responses we received from friends and family varied greatly. Some were thrilled, some shared their concerns over how close in age our youngest two would be and others actually laughed at us! Everyone has their own opinion as to how far apart children should be but the reality of it is, if the Lord desires us to have a child, well then it is going to happen no matter the precautions!

My first prenatal appointment was great, and the pregnancy progressed just like my other ones. Around 10 weeks along I started spotting and became a bit apprehensive as to what that meant. I know it is usually never good when bleeding happens during pregnancy and knowing I was still under the "safe zone" of twelve, weeks I immediately called my doctor. She had me come in right away and did an exam to make sure everything was alright. As I lay there a bit fearful and choking back tears, my doctor was quick to inform me that she believed the bleeding was only caused by a small infection. However, to ease both of our minds, she ordered an ultrasound for the next day.

That evening was the longest evening of my life! Because I was still quite early in my pregnancy, the doctor had not been able to pick up a heartbeat on the Doppler. I was still afraid of the chance the baby was in the process of miscarrying. The next morning we were up early and dropped our children off with a babysitter. After drinking my required large amount of water an hour before the ultrasound, I felt like I was ready to burst by the time we reached the hospital, not to mention having to wait an extra fifteen to twenty minutes in the waiting room. I was on the verge of informing the receptionist I just could not wait any longer and would return with a bit less pressure in my abdomen, when the ultrasound tech called out "Wendy Carr". Finally!

We stepped into the room, and I climbed on the familiar bed. My heart was pounding as quickly as was humanly possible. The lady performing my ultrasound was incredibly sweet to us. As she applied the cold jelly on my stomach, she informed us that she would look for the heartbeat first thing. As the wand was placed on my stomach the relief I felt the moment that heartbeat came up is unexplainable. Relief washed over my body in a tremendous wave and tears filled my eyes. There was our baby, healthy, growing and mighty wiggly! The tech looked at me and said, "you know, he's probably a boy! Boys usually are the cause of all this ruckus! He just wanted some attention." We smiled at her and said, "Well, he certainly has our attention now!" Little did we know, he really was a boy, and we would discover that in a way we never thought we would.

The rest of the ultrasound was pure enjoyment. Being able to observe our little peanut moving all over the place brought peace and our fears were put to rest. Thank you again, Lord! So far he was a healthy baby! By the time we left the appointment our minds were calmed and we were proudly oohing and awing over the pictures we were handed of our sweet baby. We were convinced he was one of the cutest babies around!

When all of this took place, we were in the midst of planning a big move across the country. In April of 2010, my husband made a change in jobs, and we made the move from our home in Indiana to Arizona for a wonderful ministry opportunity. My husband had been offered a job as a youth pastor, and we were thrilled! Having grown up in the West, part of my heart has always been out there. The mountains are what won me over! I remember when I was in high school looking at the views I had on the way to school each morning and thinking "I'm going to miss this when I'm at college!" Little did I know I would not be back living in mountainous country for a good ten years!

As my husband settled into his job, we began the hunt for a home of our own. We were living in a rental home and could not wait be the proud owners of our very first house. We put in a few different offers and were waiting to hear back from any one of them. We were enjoying life and loving where God had placed us in ministry. The future looked so bright! Never in our wildest dreams could we have imagined what was about to take place.

Chapter Four

When The Lord Took Away, Again

*I*t was a Wednesday night. As we headed off to youth group, the night was beautiful. The weather was perfect and the kids were happy about getting some nursery time in! After all, there was an amazing slide in that room and what child does not enjoy some quality slide time? As we pulled into our usual parking space, we saw several families who had arrived just moments before us walking up to the church building. We unbuckled the kid's car seats and dropped them off at the nursery, and my husband and I made our way down the hallway to the youth room nothing seemed out of the ordinary. There were teens milling around outside the room in the hall as usual, and our evening with the teens went well! After youth group we were able to visit some with other church folks and head back home around 9p.m. Wednesday nights were pretty busy for us and after leaving church our goal was to get our kids in bed as quickly as possible once we arrived home. Partially for their sanity, but mainly for ours! They were both pretty exhausted and falling apart at the seams by the time we got them to bed. After they were safely nestled in their respective beds for the night I took myself off to the restroom.

My husband popped his head in the door to tell me something cute Emma had just said to him as he kissed her good-night, and it was then I informed my husband of what I had found. My undergarments were covered in blood. Not enough to soak through what I had been wearing, but enough to send up an alarm in my own mind. Ever the optimist, my sweet husband informed me it was probably nothing but that we would err on the side of caution and would see a doctor in the morning. I tried not to worry as we readied ourselves for bed, but every possible "what if" managed to cross through my mind. I knew I had not felt the baby moving much since the previous week, but that also was not uncommon for how far along I was. Eighteen weeks is still considered pretty early to be feeling strong movements all the time. As my mind raced, I tried to fall asleep.

The next morning I was up early and called a doctor's office that had been recommended to us. Having just moved across country not even two weeks ago, we had not had the time to search out a doctor yet. The phone rang and on the other end a female voice cheerfully answered, "Hello?" "I need to see a doctor today, it is really important." I choked out. "Alright, what seems to be the problem?" she replied. "I am 18 weeks pregnant and I started bleeding last night" I stated. As the appointment was set up the earliest I could get in was 9:30 that morning. Immediately, I went into "mommy mode" and got the kids up and ready. We made a phone call to our new pastor to see if his wife could watch our kids for us during the appointment. Chad informed them of what was going on and through concerned voices they informed us they would watch our little ones. The 20 minute drive over to their house seemed to last forever. Every minute seemed to be drawn out.

Our Pastor and his wife assured us that our kids would be well taken care of and that they would be praying for us. They asked the usual questions of "how far along are you?" and "have you had problems with the rest of your pregnancies?" After answering their questions we headed out the door thanking them so much for being willing to watch our children at the last minute. Chad and I buckled ourselves in the van and took off for the doctor. My heart was pounding, and I was again trying to not worry but trust that the Lord knows what is best. We found a parking spot right up front and walked in the door hand in hand.

We made it to the 3rd floor, and as we were stepping out of the elevator, another lady who was also in the elevator looked at our somber faces and said "don't look so excited". I turned to my husband as if to say, "If she only knew". Walking up to the counter the receptionist handed me a clipboard of all the papers I needed to sign. Since we did not have our new insurance set up yet, she informed us that we would have to pay up front today. Not a problem, just tell me my baby is alright, I thought. After a twenty minute wait, a nurse called us back to our room. I sat on the exam table and answered all of her questions in almost robotic tones. Once she was satisfied with all of our answers, she left the room and I felt chilled nearly to the bone. The wait for the doctor to appear was not easing my nerves. I just wanted answers!

I do not honestly recall how long we waited because my mind was consumed with my baby and silent prayers. When the doctor made her appearance she also asked rather similar questions to what I had just been asked. It was then she informed us that they do not handle ob patients. WHAT?! I thought. Why, was I not told this on the phone?! I was feeling rather emotional and just about beside myself! In the calmest voice I could muster I asked "do you have a Doppler so we can at least try to hear the heartbeat?" She looked at me and said, "we do not have a Doppler, I can check but I am pretty sure we do not have any since we do not handle ob patients." My heart plummeted. That was the reason I set up this appointment. We needed to hear that sweet pounding heart in my womb. She decided to do an exam and true to what I had said, she saw blood on the swabs. Not a lot, but it was there. She told us that she would set up an ultrasound for us at another location and that brought some relief. Seeing our baby would be even better than just hearing the heartbeat, though at the moment that is all I wanted to hear!

As the doctor walked out of the room Chad and I locked eyes. Mine were filled with tears and his were full of compassion mixed with concern. We tried to remain positive, but my heart already knew something was very, very wrong. We waited in that small room for nearly 45 minutes before a nurse came back in to inform us we had an appointment set up for the ultrasound but that it would not be until 2 in the afternoon. By the time we left, it was already noon and with two kids that needed naps this just was not going to work. We thanked the nurse and walked out. As we got farther down the hall and closer to our vehicle, the tears that were caught in my throat through the entire visit spilled out with great force. I clutched the hand of my husband as we walked and I sobbed, "I just want to know my baby is alright! Why didn't they tell us on the phone they don't see ob patients?! Now we have to wait even longer to know our baby is alright!" He was just as upset as I was, though not nearly as emotional.

Chad opened my door for me, and I slid in as the tears continued to stream down. We held hands and Chad prayed for both the baby and me. We were clinging to our Great Physician! On the drive over to pick up our children I tried to compose myself. I did not want to let on that I had been crying or how upset I really was about the doctor's office not being honest with us up front. As we rang the door bell, we knew that those waiting on the other side were hoping for some good news. We walked in and informed them that we still knew nothing but that an ultrasound was scheduled for later that day. Our Pastor's wife told us she would watch the children for us once again when it was time for the ultrasound. A sweet and thoughtful gesture, but we felt terrible because we knew she had already scheduled an outing for that afternoon. "Not a problem" she replied kindly. With that it was settled. We walked out each snugly holding onto our precious children. As we drove down the road, we decided to pick up a quick lunch and try to get our little ones in bed for a nap as quickly as possible. The time seemed to drag on while we waited for the time of our appointment, and as soon as our babysitter pulled up, we rushed off.

Prayers were prayed between Chad and I all afternoon. We were literally begging God to let us hear good news. Pleading with Him to let our hearts be prepared for whatever the results would be and that through it all, He would be glorified. At times I did not even know what to say to God, but I knew He knew my heart and all the words that I did not know how to voice. Through everything going on, in the midst of my fear, there was a peace still surrounding my heart.

It was a peace that could only be described as given by the Lord. Isaiah 26:3 says,

"Thou wilt keep him in perfect peace, whose mind is stayed on thee: because he trusteth in thee."

Even in the midst of our turmoil, we were doing our best to keep our mind on Christ and He continued to pour out His peace through it all.

Silence mixed with tears was the only thing that could be heard all the way to the radiologist's office. My body had grown cold again, and I fought the urge to shiver. As we got out of the car, I looked up at the tall building and willed for the people inside to give us some good news. The elevator took us up to the 2nd floor and again we filled out paperwork. Waiting only fifteen minutes, a nurse took us back to the exam room. The room was dimly lit and had several machines in it. "Go ahead and lie down on the table," she instructed me. As I readied myself for the exam, my heart was beating so hard I was fairly certain it might come right out of my chest.

The machine was turned on, some information was given, and the gel was distributed on my slightly swollen abdomen. The screen was turned slightly away, but I strained to view what she was seeing. Immediately my own heart plummeted. I did not see the beating heart that usually pops up on the screen. As the nurse changed images to find where the blood was flowing through the baby, the colors did not change like they normally should. Having had 2 other children and having seen those colors change I knew something was wrong. I looked at her more in desperation than anything else and said "Please tell me you see a heartbeat". She gave me a slight smile, never making eye contact and replied, "I need to get the radiologist. She is going to want to take some measurements." With that she walked out of the room. I looked at Chad with fear in my eyes and said, "She never answered my question". He nodded his head in agreement, a serious expression on his face. The radiologist returned with the nurse and in hushed tones began telling her to show her different angles of the baby and such. I looked at her and again asked, "Please tell me you see a heartbeat." I'll never forget the look on her face as she shook her head no and replied, "We do not." The overwhelming sobs that shook my body were filled with instant grief. They were uncontrollable. My hands covered my face as I sobbed. I do not remember having the gel wiped off my stomach. I do not remember being put in a sitting position. I do remember the arms of my husband embracing me. He wept along with me. This grief seemed too great a weight to carry. The next thing I knew I was being asked questions about who my doctor was. I tried to feebly explain that I did not have a doctor yet, we had not even been in the area for two weeks! So the next step was to try and get in touch with the doctor I had seen earlier that morning. My body began to feel numb and it felt like a part of me had just died.

Chapter Five

Completely Heartbroken

After a few minutes that seemed like an eternity, the shock came like a wave over our bodies. The doctor and nurse stepped out of the room so as to give us some privacy and to compose ourselves a bit. I sat there on the table, staring straight ahead of me at the shadows on the wall. Guilt completely surrounded me. Without thinking, I said what was honestly in my heart, "I can't believe another one of our children is gone. I can't believe this is happening in my body." Chad enveloped me in his arms and turned my tear stained face to his own grief stricken face. He said with only love in his voice, "Honey, look at me, this is not your fault. Please, don't blame yourself." As I looked in his eyes I replied, "how can I not? This happened in my body. My body was incapable of sustaining this life!" He reminded me ever so gently that it was God's doing. It had nothing to with me or my body. Even though I knew this in my head, it was my heart that had trouble accepting it. I could not see past the realty that it did in fact happen in my body, therefore, I assumed it had something to do with me or something I had done. I had just read about how stress during pregnancy can release a hormone that can cause a miscarriage or death of a child in utero. Heaven knows we had all been under a great deal of stress for the past 6 weeks or so.

We decided we needed to share this new found information with our parents. We made phone calls to family because we needed their support, and we also knew things would probably happen quickly. We would need someone to come out on short notice to take care of our two small children. As we each relayed the news to our respective parents, the words spilled out as the tears came down. I remember saying, "We have one more child in Heaven," and I could not say another word, my tears were too great. My own mom cried with me on the phone and informed me over and over "I'll be there if you need me, just say the word." I remember hearing

Chad inform his parents and the heartbreak I heard in his voice was most unbearable. I wrapped my arms around him and listened to the explanation he relayed to his parents. It was news no one ever wants to have to share. After we hung up the phone, we sat in silence, still in the doctor's office. I looked at my husband and said, "I'm not angry with God, but this hurts so much." Knowing that God does all things for our good can be a hard truth to remember in the midst of a trial.

A few years previously when my father passed away suddenly, our Pastor came over as soon as he heard the news to be an encouragement and to pray with us. He shared with us that sometimes when events take place in our lives that seem negative, our first reaction is to say, "why is God doing this to me?" The reality of it is, God does everything *for* us. In Psalm 57:2 the Psalmist wrote:

"I will cry unto God most high; unto God that performeth all things for me."

Then again in Romans 8:28 we are told,

"And we know that all things work together for good to them that love God, to them who are the called according to his purpose."

Every event in our lives, whether viewed as positive or negative provides us an opportunity to allow God to use it for good. Even when the situation seems absolutely terrible, God wants to use it for our good and His glory. In His sovereignty Christ allows different events to take place to in each of our lives simply to draw us closer to Himself and bring glory to Him. Yes, even when our world was crashing in around us because of devastating news that our child was no longer living, God wanted to use that very event to bring us closer to Him. So there we were faced with the greatest loss of our lives and a decision to make. Were we going to allow God to use this to draw us closer to Him or use it as an excuse to run away from Him?

After approximately fifteen minutes, the nurse returned and asked, "How are you doing? Are you ok?" Ok? Not at all were we ok and we replied, "Not really, but we are surviving." She then went on to inform us that they had tried without success to reach the doctor I had seen just that morning. She said the nurses at the other office told her the soonest she could get in touch with the doctor would be the next morning. She looked at us and stated in a firm tone, "I told them that was unacceptable". She told us she would try again and be back in a few minutes. Those minutes were so long. I could not get out of my mind the thought that I was carrying my lifeless child around inside of me. The grief, it was so heavy.

The nurse re-entered the room and informed us she again had no success in talking with the doctor. We informed her that we would try to get in touch with her ourselves and with that we gathered our few belongings and left the room. Together, hand in hand we walked to the elevator.

The ride down was silent. We stepped out on the bottom floor and a man was there waiting to get on. I am sure he wondered what the problem was when he saw our tears. We slipped into our vehicle, and there I dialed the number to the doctor's office. How would I get through the conversation I had to have? Tears were numerous, and I could barely speak! A nurse answered, and as I tried to explain the situation, the words became few as the lump in my throat hindered me from doing anything but crying. The nurse on the other end was so kind and informed me that she had experienced a similar loss a few years back. She then put me through to the doctor. I do not know if it was my emotional roller coaster or if it was reality, but the doctor did not seem to know what she was talking about. Honestly though, how could she know. Dealing with O.B. patients was not her area of expertise! She put me back through to the nurse who was instructed to give me a recommendation for an O.B. She referred me to her own doctor and as soon as I hung up the phone, I dialed the number.

"Hello, Dr____'s office" the voice said on the other end of the phone. I tried to give a brief explanation, "Hi, I just recently moved here and I have no doctor. I just found out that my baby, who I am 18 weeks pregnant with, has died. I need an appointment as soon as possible." I was put through to speak with a nurse. Again I explained our situation.

"Do you have insurance?" she asked. "No, not yet. My husband just started a job and the paperwork has not yet been completed," I replied. "Well, before you can be seen by the doctor we need you to make an appointment so we can figure out how you are going to pay for the services performed."

Whoa! I was completely blindsided by the calloused answer. Without a second thought I blurted out, "You want me to make an appointment to talk about money instead of letting me see the doctor to get this taken care of?" I could not help it. The words just tumbled out. I was hurt and offended. The lack of compassion, though probably not intentional, was too much for me at the time. The nurse tried to be kind, "Well, ma'am I know this is a very sensitive and emotional time for you, but we need to know how we are going to be paid." Again, the lack of compassion felt like a slap in the face. Forget it. I could not talk about this right now. I told her I would have to call her back later on. It was then she informed me that I would not even be able to see the doctor until late the next week. What?! This was sounding more and more ridiculous! I hung up the phone and cried. I told my husband, "I have a baby inside of me that is no longer living, and all they want to talk about is MONEY?!" The situation seemed to become even more hopeless, and we had no idea what to do next because we could not get a doctor to even see me all because I had no insurance.

By the time we arrived back home I had tried to compose myself. Our Pastor's wife had already been informed of what was going on and she was very compassionate. She spoke very encouragingly, and we thanked her up and down for watching our children a good portion of the day. She then left us to return to her own home and we needed figure out what we were going to do. Chad decided to go pick up the few things we needed from the store, and he took both of our children with him to give me some much needed time alone. When he left I decided to write a blog entry and update my readers on what was taking place. I had a private family blog at the time and writing was my way of releasing my raging thoughts. With every word I typed about the events that were taking place, I poured my heart out to that keyboard. Every little click of the keys brought tears streaming down my face. My entry that evening read,

> *"Broken-hearted, that describes our hearts right now. We headed to get an ultrasound done and as soon as the baby came on the screen I had a feeling and it wasn't a good one. Having carried this baby for 18 weeks now, feeling the flutters and watching my waistline expand slowly all caused us to grow in anticipation of the upcoming arrival of baby number 4. Now all of those dreams have been shattered!*
>
> *One of the first thoughts that entered my mind was, "Lord, I always have told you whatever it takes to keep me tender towards you, that is what I want. I am not mad at you but I surely am hurting and grieving for this baby."*

Honestly, in my heart of hearts, there is no anger or bitterness, just hurt and an ache to know this child that left us all to soon in our opinion. Eighteen weeks, so small and yet it amazes me at how far the developmental process has brought him/her.

It is strange to know that there is still a baby in my womb that no longer has a beating heart. A child that is already in the presence of Christ. I think it would be that much harder if we didn't have our faith and truly believe that to be absent from the body is to be present with the Lord. How are we doing? Chad has shed tears, his heart is broken and yet he is so strong. He has been so compassionate and loving. My tears are constant and words are few. What is there to say? I think we are both still in a state of shock. A heavy heavy heart is in my chest and a desire to hold my baby even just once is so strong I cannot even describe. So here I sit, rocking away, rocking the baby that is in my womb for only a few short more days and wishing that baby could be in my arms. Desiring for him/her to KNOW that we love him/her so much. Wishing he/

she didn't have to leave my womb in such a way. Thankful that the Lord knows what He is doing praying for the faith that is needed to trust that He knows what is best.

God does all things for our good and for His glory. Our hope and prayer is that we come through this with a stronger faith and with an even deeper knowledge of the compassionate Savior He is. We pray that as we go through this time of grief that when other see us they see the love and compassion of Christ. He is going to get us through. In a post only a month ago I remember writing "sometimes life hurts, sometimes it REALLY hurts and right now it is REALLY hurting." We appreciate and covet your prayers. We will press on, one day at a time. Please pray that we will have wisdom as to what to do next. How to get this all taken care of. Thank you so much.

Sweet baby mine, I love you more than words can describe. The tears that are constantly spilling over are all for you and the grief I am experiencing right now. You are one loved little person and you are making heaven sound all the more sweeter. Your daddy loves you and has shed tears for you as well. I can't help but feel partial blame for this. Though I know the Lord knows what is best, my mind sometimes gets the better of me and I feel at fault in some way because this happened to you in my body. I wish I could just hold you, rock you, snuggle you close and tell you just how much I love you. For now, I'll have to let the Lord do so. He knows how to take better care of you than I do, I know you are in perfect and capable hands. Save your mommy a seat next to you, don't get to big to fast and when I reach Heaven one day, make sure those arms are open wide because your mommy is for sure going to come and give you the most gigantic hug ever known! You have good company up there, that brother/sister of yours is just as sweet as you are I'm sure. Oh how I love you. I wish there was a stronger word than "love" to describe how I feel about you. I suppose that earthly word will have to do for now. Can't wait to see you whole and healthy one day!

Love,
Mommy"

I seemed to be standing still while the rest of the world raced by. I did not understand, I had so many questions I did not know how to voice, and as I typed, I rocked in the arm chair. I remember thinking, "I'm rocking my baby for one of the last times. The only time I will be able to rock him is in my womb." This was a grief I had never known, a grief that was so deep and nearly suffocating.

When my husband arrived home, we made the kids dinner. While everyone was eating, I retreated to our bedroom and soaked my pillow with even more tears. Chad would pop in and check on me, and I could hear sweet Emma asking, "Is Mommy ok?" Chad was more than wonderful as he really took over from there for the evening. The kids were changed into their pajamas and still I lay there swallowed up in grief. I could not muster the energy to rise from the bed. "God, where are you?" I asked again and again. My husband brought the kids in to see me and I kissed them good-night and hugged them extra tight. I needed their good-night kisses and hugs more than they knew. I thanked God right then and there for our two healthy and happy children. The Lord had been good to us. He had blessed us beyond measure. I knew that this was a valley, but it was a tough valley.

That evening a song came into my head and it stuck with me throughout the many weeks that followed. The words go something like this:

Through the tears I want to trust you through my tears,
Though the pain seems more than I can bear.
At times it seems I'm blind, and answers are so hard to find.
Lord, hear my cry, help me trust you through my tears.[1]

Though it was so hard, I wanted SO MUCH to trust the Lord through this whole situation. I wanted to trust that His way really was perfect. When trials come I truly believe that is when the rubber meets the road as to where our faith really lies. It can be so easy to blame God, to get angry with Him and to shake our fist in His face while demanding all the answers. Yet, when everything is going smoothly, it is also very easy to forget Him. Where does our faith really lie? I kept repeating in my mind, "God is good all the time and all the time God is good". I really did and still do believe it but God seemed silent.

[1] Nickel, Karey and Kelly. New Mercy. Karey and Kelly Nickel. © 2000 by Nickel Music.CD.

The night droned on. Chad was ready for bed long before I was. Though I had been up early and hardly slept the night before, sleep eluded me. Once he went to bed I remember going into the living room, literally getting on my knees and crying out audibly "God, this seems too much! I can't handle this grief! I am not strong enough to go through this trial!" Sobs wracked my body from the very core of my being. A grief like this was something new to me, and all I could do was pour out my broken heart to God. He sat there with me, I know He did. His heart was broken for me. It felt like I could almost feel God's arms of love wrapped around me. Like a loving Father does, He wiped my tears, listened to the prayer of my heart that became so deep I could not even voice it. He knew. He knew what I wanted to say but was unable put into words.

Once the tears stopped pouring, I stood up, walked back to my bedroom and crawled into bed. As I lay there, next to my husband, I put my hand on my stomach. I could still feel my baby's little body in there. The tears returned and as I tried my best to cry in hushed tones so as not to wake my husband, the Lord was still there. He never left my side. I have never cried so much in all of my life! Sleep did eventually come out of pure exhaustion, but I woke around 4 the next morning. All I wanted to do was pray and write. I had to get my thoughts out of my head and onto paper. So I returned to my computer screen and began to type once again.

Eventually the rest of the family began waking up, and we got ready for the un-deniably difficult day. I began once again making several phone calls to different OB offices. Since I did not have an OB because of our recent move, it was left on my shoulders to try and find one. After several phone calls to different offices, the tears started flowing again. I felt like no one cared, no one wanted to help. They would not even let me set up an appointment! I felt like I had something terribly wrong with me, and no one even wanted to touch me. They all kept repeating the same information, "Go to the hospital. Let them do an ultrasound to confirm what you have told us, and they will take care of it." No matter how many times I told them I had already had an ultrasound, they did not seem to hear me.

I sobbed into the chest of my husband and tried to explain my frustration over what was going on and what they all had told me, and he decided to take over. After helping to calm me down, he picked up the phone and called the radiologist office that we were just at the day before. He explained the situation and what the result of our ultrasound showed. He then explained that we needed a copy of the ultrasound to take to the hospital. The lady on the other end of the line was more than helpful and informed Chad that usually it takes up to 3 working days to get a copy of the ultrasound but that she would be sure to have it ready for us within the hour.

A gracious couple in our new church offered to watch our children for us during our visit to the hospital. Once we dropped the kids off, we drove in silence to the hospital. All that could be heard at times were the sniffles coming from my side of our vehicle. My husband reached over and held my hand the entire trip. He was so strong and provided the security I needed. When we pulled into the parking lot, I grabbed the envelope that contained the precious ultrasound pictures of my baby and knew these would be the last pictures I would ever have of this precious baby. We walked up to the information desk and for lack of knowing exactly how to word what needed to be said I exclaimed, "I am 18 weeks pregnant and found out my baby is no longer living. I do not know where to go," I blurted out. The elderly lady at the information desk looked surprised and sent us to the 3rd floor, O.B. triage. When we stepped out of the elevator, we walked right up to the counter and informed the receptionist what was going on. In hushed tones she helped us fill out our paperwork. It was tremendously hard not to notice the rather large pregnant belly of the lady sitting next to us. It took everything in me to not reach over and tell her, "Do you know what a miracle you have in there?" Instead, the tears blurred my vision and I kept still.

We were led into the triage where I was weighed and given a room. The curtained walls did not keep out the sounds of the other ladies in there. It did not keep out the healthy beating heartbeats that could be heard on the monitors. "Here is a gown, I will be back in a few minutes," the nurse instructed. When she returned, she asked all the questions that usually take place in a triage.....well, most of them anyway. We informed her we had the ultrasound from the day before, and she took it with her to show to the doctor. I am not sure how long we waited, but it was long enough to know neither one of us wanted to be there that was for sure. The doctor eventually came in. He was a young looking man who was just finishing up his residency. He informed us that he had read over our ultrasound and report and after asking us how we were doing, he began to explain our options.

Option number one was to wait. I could go home and wait it all out to see if my body would deliver the baby on its own. Knowing what the radiologist had told us the day before, the doctor then reiterated that even if we decided to wait it out at home, we eventually would come back and have to go through this all anyway. Why drag it out? Our second option was to do a d & e. "You would go to an abortion clinic where they do this all the time. Your baby is too big to do a d & c, so they would do a d & e where he would not come out whole." He lost my interest as soon as he mention "abortion clinic". Once he was done with that option, I told him this was not an option at all in our opinion, "I will not let my baby be all cut up. I can promise you that is not going to happen." I understand he was only doing what he had been trained to do, but what mother would want to choose that for her child? It did not matter that our baby had no heartbeat. He was not going to be chopped up as if I could have cared less about him! Our third, and only option in our minds, was to induce labor. So, the prep work for that option began to take place. The doctor explained that they would insert something into my cervix to start dilation. I could go home, at my request, and come back in the morning to have my progress checked. If I had dilated enough they would insert a pill that would start my contractions.

The items were inserted and the doctor left. While we waited to be let go, we called our families and informed them that we needed someone to come out as soon as possible to take care of our kids during my hospital stay. After checking calendars and pricing, my mom was able to come out that night. We could not have been more appreciative! Being in a new town and not really knowing anyone, it did my own heart good knowing a relative would be caring for our children. It was decided that I would stay home with the kids and get them off to bed while Chad and our Pastor went to pick up my mom. While they were out, I spent some time praying, reading my Bible and updating the blog once again.

"The hardest part is still to come. To me, as of right now, the hardest part of this all will be to deliver the baby and have to leave the hospital without my baby. Never seeing him again. Even as I write this my tears are so great in number. I do not feel strong

enough to endure this and yet here we are. I remember hearing stories of friends and strangers having to go through this process and really admiring the woman involved. I thought 'wow, she has got to be so strong' when in actuality, though she probably was a lot stronger than I, she was probably just like me. Feeling the weight of this burden was far heavier than she could carry. Wondering how she would get through it all. Scared to ever think about having another child fearing this would happen again. Aching to hold the child. It is a dark valley to cross through, that is for sure.

Once our baby is delivered, which will probably happen sometime tomorrow if all goes according to plan, we will be given the choice of seeing our baby. The nurses would clean the baby up and hand him to us in a towel if we so choose. Never did I think that at 28 years of age I would be burying one of my own children. Oh the heartbreak. To have to bury your own child is not something any parent should have to go through. It is SO hard, I cannot tell you. After the baby comes it could be another

6–8 hrs. before the placenta delivers, if it does deliver. It has a chance that it may not because the placenta knows it isn't time for it to come out and it is probably pretty strongly attached to the uterine wall. If it doesn't deliver within the approximate time range then I will have to have a d and c done to get it out. Boy this is tough.

Chad has been amazing. He has been such a comfort and has told me how he wishes he could do this all for me. Funny, I wouldn't want to see him in the pain that I am in and will go through in the coming days. I would rather take it than see him go through it all. I suppose that is what love is about isn't it. I personally am having a rough time. Sleep evades me though I feel completely exhausted. In its stead are a multitude of tears. As the items to help me dilate were inserted I just cried through the entire process. I don't want to be going through this! Inside I truly feel dead. Like a part of me has died along with this child. I feel tremendous guilt that somehow I did something that caused all of this to happen. My mind plays tricks on me and sometimes I think I can feel the baby move. I think sometimes that if the baby just stays inside that somehow miraculously the baby will come back to life. Maybe it is denial, maybe it is all a part of the grieving process. I just know that a part of my heart has died and will forever be with my child.

My mom is flying in tonight which will be a great help and comfort I know. I know that I will be at peace during my stay at the hospital knowing that my kids are well taken care of. The Dr. wanted to keep me in the hospital all during the dilation process but I requested to come home to be with my kids. Now that my mom will be here it is a worry put to rest. Chad's parents will be flying in late next week.

As we go through each step of this painful process it honestly feels too great a load to carry. Yet, the Lord's grace is sufficient. He gives us the grace and compassion we need to get through the next step. We are clinging to His promise that He is walking through this valley of the death of our child. Do I call it a miscarriage? No. I will be delivering this baby and to me that is no miscarriage. My child has died. Died. On the way to the hospital I thought about the Lord and how He sent His ONLY Son to die on a cross for me. His grief was far more than mine I am sure. If I am getting a small taste of what the Father felt when His Son died, oh how it makes me appreciate my salvation more. There has been a chorus to a song stuck in my head since early this morning. The words are "through the tears, I want to trust you through my tears. Though the pain seems more than I can bear. At times it seems I'm blind and answers are so hard to find. Lord hear my cry, Help me trust You through the tears." The prayer of my heart right now.

Sweet baby mine, I love you so much!"

When my mom and Chad made it home, it was a comfort to me to see my mom walk in the door. With all the tears that had been shed, my eyes were so swollen and puffy and my mom just hugged me and cried. After a few minutes we made our way into the kitchen. I sat and wrote out a schedule for our kids for my mom. It was the first time that she would be staying with them over night without us around, and we wanted our kids to stay on a normal schedule. Afterwards I tried to explain it all to her, and she assured me that they would be in good hands. Then came the explanation in more detail as to what was going to take place in the morning. The medicine was working, I could already feel the contractions beginning as my body prepared for the premature delivery of our baby.

Chapter Six

Waiting For His Arrival

We talked until after 10 that night and then turned in for the night. As I readied myself for bed, I decided to take some medicine that the doctor had given me. It was supposed to help with the pain of contractions and help me sleep. Wouldn't you know it, that night our youngest little guy decided to wake up several times. My poor groggy husband was the one that had to take care of him because I was loopy from the medicine! The next morning we got up and readied ourselves for the day. Neither of us wanted this day to happen. I cried almost all morning long. I looked at my husband and said, "I don't want to do this," and I meant it with all of my heart!

Before we left, I took the time to write out a blog entry, bearing the deepest thoughts of my heart.

*written May 1st

This is the day, the day when our baby will make his appearance. I will hold my baby for the first time, and for the last. It doesn't seem fair, in a way that everyone else's life is going forward. As we drive down the road I see people cheerfully chatting on the phone, others enjoying the company of friends and family and right now, it just seems so wrong. I don't expect that life for everyone else will stop because of what we are going through, but in a way it really really seems like it should. Selfish thoughts, probably.

All night I felt the beginnings of labor. Even as I type this, the labor pains are *attacking* my body. The loosening joints that are now sore from loosening up so quickly. The contractions that have now begun are a constant reminder that my child, which has no life left in him, is coming out. Today. Today will be a day I will remember the rest of my life. It will be a remembrance of how the grace of

God was proven over and over to be sufficient. That doesn't mean my heart isn't breaking. That doesn't mean I don't wish for some miraculous healing and life to be given back to my baby. Today is the day I remember that my children are not really mine, but they truly are God's. Today is the day I truly realize that the Lord's thoughts are certainly higher than my own and that He will be a better caregiver than I could ever wish to be.

This child will never know the sin of this world. This child will forever get to live his life for the glory of God without the battle of sin lurking in the background. This child, my sweet sweet child will be waiting for me when it is my turn to enter Heaven's gates. I am thankful my children have each other to keep them company in Heaven, along with several cousins.

My tears are numerous. Some have been shed in secret. Some have been shed in the wee morning hours as I lie awake waiting for the dawn. Tears have been shed while my husband and I cling to each other and others have been shed while we hold hands and pray together. The day that is ahead will not be an easy one, but I am so thankful to be able to go through this with my godly, loving, compassionate husband by my side. I am a proud mommy of FOUR, out of this world beautiful children.

Today. Weeping may endure for today, but joy will come, we cling to that promise. God is good all the time and all the time God is good."

I closed my laptop. We said our tearful good-byes to our children all the while trying to protect them from knowing any of the pain that was in our hearts, and we headed out the door to make our appointment at 10. On the way we called my in-laws and the tears could not be held back. I remember getting on the phone with my father in-law and just sobbed, "I don't want to do this! I just don't want to do it!" His comforting, "I know. We are praying for you," was so loving. I know it was difficult for them to be so far away knowing what a heartbreaking time it was for us. Hearing how much people were praying for us was an indescribable comfort though.

As we pulled into the parking garage at the hospital the tears would not stop. When we stepped in the elevator my tears seemed to just come even harder. Stepping out on the same floor we had yesterday was all too familiar. We walked up to the receptionist and informed her I had an appointment. She looked from my face to my nearly flat stomach, back to my face and back to my stomach with a confused look on her face. I quietly explained, "My baby has died, and I am here to deliver him." Understanding washed over her face as she grabbed some papers behind her, and she asked, "What was your name?" "Wendy," I replied quietly. "Aww, yes" and the paperwork began to be filled out. She looked up at me again and said, "You have such an angelic face". I was taken aback. I replied, "Thank you, I don't feel angelic though. My heart is full of sadness." She looked at me and said, "I'm old you know, my youngest is 32 and by now, I can tell when someone has a beautiful soul and you have it. It is shown on your face." It must have been the Lord she was seeing, and I am thankful that even though all I felt was grief, she could still see a reflection of Christ shining through.

Once the paperwork was filled out, we went back into the triage again and were put in the same room as the day before. There were two expectant ladies in their own curtained rooms. One of which thought she was in labor, but by the laughter I heard coming from behind the curtain, I knew she could not possibly be in labor. If you are in true labor, nothing really seems funny! The sounds of healthy baby heartbeats were heard down the short hallway and surprisingly, it was not painful to hear. Honestly, I was happy for those women and would not desire my own situation on them. When the nurse came to do the normal preliminaries, we questioned her as to what the hospital does by way of memorabilia. She was incredibly kind and patient to us as she explained what they have for people in our situation. She became teary eyed when I started sobbing half way through her explanation. I felt badly for making her cry, but it was also sweet to see her tender compassionate heart.

The doctor came in about 45 minutes later. After some quick checking, he was pleased with what he discovered. He could see and feel my bag of water bulging. A good sign that the medicine had been doing its job. While the doctor was checking my progress, I began shaking uncontrollably. My body was already in shock. The tears could not be held back as he explained the rest of the what was about to take place. When he left, I tried my best to compose myself. I did not want those other ladies to hear the tears of my grief. Not something they needed to hear in the midst of their joy.

I was wheeled away on my hospital gurney to the maternity ward. Small smiles were exchanged as we passed hospital staff in the hall. My heart only grew heavier the closer we got to the maternity ward. As soon as we entered my delivery room, the tears I fought so hard to contain started back up. I saw the basinet sitting in the room, the one that normal healthy babies are placed on to get cleaned up and examined. My baby would not be placed in there for all of those exams. Oh the ache in my soul was deep. I escaped to the restroom to try to compose myself, but the tears kept coming. I stood there weeping into my hands and begged the Lord for His strength to endure this time. After several minutes I tried to compose myself as best I could and climbed back into my hospital bed.

The doctor arrived a few minutes later, and the medicine was given to start the contractions. After a few encouraging words and a promise to return, he left the room. A nurse brought in several papers which needed to be signed and a death certificate had already been prepared. "We don't have a name picked out yet" we explained to the nurse. "That is alright, we can wait to fill that part out," she kindly replied. After the nurse left the room with the certificate Chad and I did some investigating for names. We wanted a first and middle name that had a deep meaning, a meaning that signified what was going on in life right then. We browsed through different websites, both of us finding this task to be rather difficult. What do you name your child who has already passed into eternity? I strongly believe the Lord led us right to the names we needed to choose and both of us really liked them.

As time passed on we held hands and simply waited. Neither of us had any words to say, but holding each other was all that we needed right then. We were overwhelmed with the responses, e-mails and phone calls from those who were really praying for us. We appreciated the words of encouragement and the tears shed on our behalf. As we began the process that would eventually lead to our son being born, we were amazed at the peace that was surpassing our understanding. God has been good in our life. The day that seemed impossible was met with grace more than sufficient to help us in our time of need.

Chapter Seven

Face To Face Meeting With Eli

As the hours passed, it was becoming more evident to me that the baby would come soon. The contractions were definitely getting stronger as I began to dilate. The doctor had already informed us that our baby would be tiny and would probably be born without any doctors or nurses in the room. That scared me. I was not sure if I would be able to handle that situation if it did happen. Around 6p.m., the doctor made his appearance once again to check my progress. Just before he had come in the room I leaned over and told my husband, "I think if he tries to put in more medicine, my water is going to break. I can just feel it." True to my thoughts, as soon as the doctor tried to put in more medicine, my water did break. The warm gush that flowed out started my heart pounding. The reality of why we were there was about to take place. Was I ready for it? My doctor then proceeded to deliver our son. There was slight tugging and then a smooth delivery.

"He's out. The baby has been delivered," he said.

My heart that was already pounding somehow got faster. I wondered what he looked like. We did not know the gender yet of our baby, so I asked quietly, "Can you tell what gender our baby is?" The doctor informed us, "He's a boy". A boy! Another son! "Now, did you want to hold your baby?" the Doctor asked. "Yes!" we replied.

We had discussed ahead of time whether or not we wanted to see and hold our son. Would it be terribly difficult? Would he be grossly deformed or decayed? Is this how we wanted to remember him? All these questions and more roamed through our minds previously, but we truly felt at peace about seeing our son. We knew if we did not we would more than likely have regret later on and also wonder, "What if we had?" Neither of those thoughts and feelings were something we wanted to deal with. So yes, we did want to see our baby.

Ever so carefully, our son was laid on a baby blanket and handed over to us. As soon as I saw him, pride swelled in my chest and I looked at my husband and said, "Look what God has created! He is beautiful!" The doctor did his best to explain everything about our son. After being examined, there was no obvious reason as to why our son had passed away in my womb, he just simply did. Once he explained all he felt he could, we were then left with our sweet boy, alone.

I remember just gazing at my son, so perfect. So beautiful! Where once there was fear as to what he would look like, now there was nothing but love. He was beautiful. He was perfect. He was my sweet baby boy! The peace that engulfed our hospital room was something that can only be explained as indescribable. My tears dried up as I just stared in awe at him, my beautiful tiny baby. Chad and I ooh'd and awed over him as most parents do their children. I looked at my husband with love and said, "Thank you for giving me such a perfect little boy. I love him!"

After some tender kisses I handed our son over to my husband and his own tears trickled down his cheeks. I looked at my husband as he held the miniature body of our baby in his hands. How does one hold a baby so tiny? A baby so small that can fit perfectly in your hand? The same way one holds a baby of normal size, with love and tenderness. The tears on my husband's face spoke more than words ever could. His heart was stricken with love and grief as he said hello and good-bye all at the same time. He had not left my side since we got to the hospital and here he sat, dealing with the greatest heartbreak he had ever had to face. During our time with our little boy, we took not nearly enough pictures, talked to our son and finally announced his name. Elioenai Matthew.

The name Elioenai means "my eyes are toward God". As we pondered that name and the meaning of it, it just seemed so fitting. Our sons eyes would only ever see the face of God! He is forever singing the praises of God, no distractions from sin, nothing. Just pure and holy reverence to our God is what our son would ever only know. What an incredible gift! We also chose his name because even through this dark valley we were walking, we yearned for our eyes to remain on Christ as well. Matthew means "gift from God" which is exactly what little Eli was. He was our gift from God. Though he was with us for only 18 all too short weeks, he was a true gift from the Lord. His little life had begun to teach us so much about God that we never knew. Would we have rather learned these truths about God in a different way? You bet we would! However, God's thoughts are much higher than our own, and His ways are unexplainable. If this is the way He has chosen to teach us about Him, there is not much we can do about it except to trust Him and learn to begin praising Him through our life's storm.

While we held our little boy we made phone calls to family, as all proud parents do. We wanted to brag on him, tell our families how perfect he was. They cried and shared in our pride and our grief. After spending only a little over an hour with him, we knew it was time. The fact of the matter was, our son's soul was not in that tiny body. It was already with Jesus, and we knew that as time went on, it would only cause his body to deteriorate and that was something we did not want to see happen. We wanted to remember him like this. Perfect. As the nurse came in to collect our son I, the forever protective mother, informed the nurse that I wanted him treated with respect and gently taken care of. Even though he was not living, I wanted his body to be treated with care. She assured me he would be well taken care of. Then

with that, she walked out of the room with our precious son. We knew we would never see him again
on this earth. A fact that broke my heart yet again
and the tears that had dried up when I held him in
my arms could not be held back any longer. How do
you say good-bye to your child? How do you handle
the harsh reality of never seeing him again on this
earth? The only thing we knew to do was to cry out
to God for help.

As promised the doctor came back in about two
hours later and needed to check the progress of my
placenta delivering. It appeared to be "stuck," and
he decided to try and help it along. I sobbed audibly
through the entire thing. The pain all seemed so
pointless. I had nothing, no living baby to show for
it. The hurt in my heart and soul cannot be written
down in words because there are none to explain
it. After 30 minutes, the doctor was able to get my
placenta out. He was very compassionate and apol-
ogized for the pain he had caused me and for what
we had just been through.

Eventually, the room cleared out of doctors and
nurses. We were alone once again. We were left to
grieve and to try to get some rest for the evening.
Giving birth to a still born was vastly different from

giving birth to a live baby. When our healthy children were born, we had visitors come to visit us and the new baby. Flowers and balloons filled the room and joy was always present! This time though no visitors came to see how we were doing. No Pastor came and prayed with us or offered words of encouragement, both of which would have been very welcome. I suppose the birth of a baby born still leaves many on the outside feeling too uncomfortable to be able to try and comfort the grieving parents. We literally felt alone. It was just my husband and I and God, for we were the only ones in the room.

Before I could fall asleep I needed to write. I just had to get my thoughts out of my mind onto paper. This is what I wrote on my blog that night:

"At 6:10 this evening on Saturday, May 1st, one of the most beautiful baby boys was born. He is perfect. He is handsome, which means he looks like his daddy! He has a perfectly formed body and I am blessed to have been able to hold his sweet body. He apparently passed into eternity sometime within the last week. Which means those little kicks I felt last week were really his. The cause of his death

is unknown. We believe though that is was so God could be magnified. His short little life is not in vain.

When my little boy was born tears were shed, but you know, true to His Word, the grace of God was waiting for us. Going through labor was worth it. Though it was painful and I thought it would be impossible, God's grace was all sufficient. His peace is SO REAL. My heart is completely at peace, as is Chad's. There is a calmness like I have never known before. I praise the Lord for His promises that are completely true.

Elioenai Matthew is his name. Elioenai means "my eyes are toward God". Perfect. My son, our son, his eyes have only seen the eyes of God. His eyes will forever be on God. No distractions. No sin. Praise the Lord and oh how I wish I could say the same for myself! We chose his name because of the meaning. We want our eyes to be toward God as well. He is a good God. He is good all the time. After seeing my son I can understand why the Lord would want him to be with Him. He is precious. Perfect. Yet, perfect. His short little life has made a big impact on us already. We pray that through all of this others would come to know Christ and that those who are not walking with God would see the importance of living for Him.

Chad is here and will be staying the night with me at the hospital. He is amazing. My heart broke when I saw the tears streaming down his face. He is a great daddy. We are grieving for our child that died but are so thankful for the grace that has carried us through. Elioenai Matthew, I love you so much. I feel honored to have been able to carry you for 18 weeks. You are a miracle and you are perfect. You have helped to make me a stronger woman and have taught me to have increased faith. You have helped to teach me to "let go" of my kids and to realize that all of you belong to Him. I thank the Lord He allowed you to be on loan to me for just a short time. I enjoyed the small kicks. I will forever cherish them. I loved being able to see your beating heart at 10 weeks and am thankful for the opportunity to have seen you a healthy thriving baby in my womb at one time.

You are a miracle. You are perfect and oh how I love you.

Love, Mommy"

The doctor had ordered some sleeping pills for me to have at my disposal if needed. After failing miserably at trying to fall asleep, I decided it would not hurt to take one. Though I was completely exhausted, my mind just would not shut off long enough for me to get some rest. As the sleeping pill began to take effect, I tried my best to just stop thinking. I closed my eyes and willed away everything from my mind.

Though I gave it my best shot, I was unable to *turn off* my brain. It kept wandering. Ever have that trouble? Thoughts about my baby boy roamed through my head at a rapid pace. Wishing he was there with us still, wondering what was going on with him, hoping he did not feel alone and so many more thoughts crossed my mind. I silently prayed that night that God would love on my little boy extra for me. That He would give him all the goodnight kisses I wished I could give him. That He would let my sweet boy know how much he was loved and how my arms had a permanent ache in them that only he could fill. Eventually the sleeping pill got the better of me and the last thing I remember that night, aside from the one last blood pressure check from the nurse, was talking with God about my son.

Chapter Eight

Leaving With Only A Box

*T*he next morning we were awakened early when the doctor came in to make sure everything was still alright, physically. He asked, "Are you in pain?" I replied quietly, "Not physically". He then began to get the papers around for my discharge from the hospital. About 9 that morning a social worker came through to ask us questions as to what we wanted done with our son's body. Is any parent ever really prepared to handle arrangements like that? I felt numb and only wanted to sob. Instead, around tremendous lumps in our throat we explained we wanted to bury little Eli. We filled out all the necessary paperwork and arrangements were made. Not complicated by any means. Just a simple swipe of the pen with our signature and it was done. He was really gone, and he was really going to be buried. The most difficult papers I have ever had to sign were that of my son's death certificate and now this.

Once the arrangements were made, we were then free to leave and go home. That was it. It was done. We came to do what we needed to do and then it was over. We gathered our things together and headed for the door. It all just felt *so wrong!* As we walked out of the room I was carrying the box full of the only mementos we would ever have of our son and it all seemed completely unfair! "A box! I came in and delivered my baby and all I have to show for it is a BOX!" I thought. As we winded our way through the halls the choking sobs that were in my throat came out. It took everything in me not to turn and run back to the nurses' station and demand they give my baby back to me. With every step forward it was one more step away from my baby whom I would never see again on this earth. The anguish of it all was overwhelming. The tears nearly blinded my eyes and caused my body to shake with sobs from the intense pain of it all. I did not care that people were looking. I did not care that the man cleaning the floors could see my broken heart coming out through the tears on my face. I just did not care. A box. That is all I had left of my son.

Quite honestly, the temptation to be angry with God at that moment was a real battle. It is hard to not have all the answers or even one answer as to why this was happening and the temptation to demand all the "why's?" be answered was so great. My intent in this book is to be real, and if I am going to be honest and vulnerable, I have to openly admit I struggled with this being part of God's plan for our life! Though I may ask the Lord "why" His answer is sometimes silence and that can be a tough pill to swallow. However, I needed to be accepting of that fact. My getting angry with the Lord would not accomplish anything.

As we stepped in the elevator my loving Chad put his arms around me. He continuously reminded me it would be alright. We climbed in our vehicle and I could not hold back what was in my heart any longer and I let loose. "It isn't FAIR! This is so WRONG! I don't WANT to leave my baby behind! I can't HANDLE THIS ANYMORE!" I sobbed. Again, he just listened and held me. It was just the reality of raw emotion in the midst of our trial. The ride home was fairly quiet apart from the hushed sniffles coming from both of us. When we pulled into the driveway, I could not wait to get in the house and hold my two perfectly healthy children. I needed their love, their hugs and kisses. When we walked in the door, we were met with all the love a parent could ever want from their little ones. Hugs came at us in full force and it was like a balm to my soul.

I willingly stepped back into mommy mode and fed my children lunch and prepared them for their afternoon naps. I needed to do that. I needed the reminder that though the greatest tragedy of our lives had just happened, I still had purpose in this life. I had a husband and children to care for and they needed me. After we put the kids down for a nap my husband and I went in the living room and as I sat on his lap, we played some encouraging songs we both love. One song in particular is written by one of my husband's favorite Southern Gospel groups, Legacy Five. It is entitled "Hello After Good-bye". As the words to the song echoed through our living room we sobbed as we clung to each other. We felt as if we had been robbed of even being able to say hello to our baby boy before he slipped into eternity. We had no answers as to why it all happened. It just did, and we were left to carry on with the unknown answers. How in the world would we survive?

This was not the first heartbreak we have had to endure, but it had been the most difficult by far. We had been taught that during the most heart-breaking of times is when it seems the Lord shines the brightest. He seems so close you could reach out and touch Him. I was determined to truly believe that God is good all the time and all the time God is so good. My circumstances should not be what determines how much or how little praise I gave to God. He is worthy of my praise at all times, even when it is incredibly difficult. Just as Philippians 4:12-13 states, *"I know both how to be abased, and I know how to abound: every where and in all things I am instructed both to be full and to be hungry, both to abound and to suffer need. I can do all things through Christ which strengtheneth me."* Christ would give us the strength we needed to keep on praising Him.

That night as I lay in bed, I opened the box that contained the memorabilia from our little boy. I held the tiny jewelry ever so gently and lovingly looked at the all too few baby pictures of him the hospital had taken. I pulled out one of his tiny baby blankets and held it tightly to my chest. I felt like a child myself as

I clung to the blanket. My little Eli had been placed on this blanket when the nurses took his picture. In some way I felt like holding his blanket would make me feel closer to him and that was a small comfort. I placed the blanket between my husband and myself that night and slept with it there. I needed to feel its presence.

The days immediately following the birth of little Eli seem like a blur. I remember the first week coming and going and wondering where the time went. I remember sorting through all the papers the hospital sent home with us. After reading over the different papers on "grief", which basically explained what to expect from each family member who was dealing with this grief, I became thankful. The problems and issues that were described on the papers made me so thankful for my husband. The explanations of why there would be marital discord and the like were poured out on the papers before me. It made me thankful that as my husband and I, clung to the Lord during that difficult time, He was in return drawing us closer together. He kept our marriage incredibly strong through the deepest of valleys. The only praise for that goes to God. He was and still is the glue that has kept our marriage strong and secure.

For several weeks I felt like I needed my husband more than ever before. I needed the security he brought me. I needed the love he gave so freely, and I needed to be held in his strong and confident arms. Though my husband was also dealing with losing his son, he really was everything I needed him to be at that time. We were already known for being a "sappy" or "hopeless romantic" type of couple, but holding his hand meant so much more to me. It simply said "I'm here," and that encouraged my heart greatly. We would pray together and read God's Word searching for encouragement. We knew that the Lord was the only one Who would be able to even begin to heal the deep wound in our hearts. There were times when we needed to get away to be just the two of us, and we were so thankful for my mom being able to watch our children while we went on much needed dates.

Throughout the day I poured over my Bible searching for encouragement. As I read different chapters and verses in Job, I knew that it was important for me to willingly give my son back to God. Even though he was already in God's presence, I personally needed to give him back to the Lord. It made me think of Hannah in the Bible. Hannah was a woman who desired to have a child and yet her womb was closed for some reason. She made the decision to take this burden of her heart to the One who knew how to handle it, and she prayed constantly for a child to be given to her. Hannah promised the Lord that if He ever chose to give her a child, she would give him back to God for His service.

One day the Lord chose to answer the cry of her heart. Hannah found out she was expecting and my mind's eye can only imagine the rejoicing she felt! Nine months later she gave birth to a beautiful baby boy, and she named him Samuel. True to her promise she gave her precious son Samuel back to the Lord. When he was old enough, Hannah took little Samuel to the temple to help the priest and serve there. From just a small little guy he served in the Lord's work.

Though mine and Hannah's stories are not similar in many regards, we do have something in common. We both prayed that if the Lord would so choose to grow our family, we would willingly give those children back to Him. The Lord took our son before he entered this world and without giving us so much as a warning to prepare us. Little Eli was so precious to us. He had forever changed our lives and there I was, faced with a choice. Do I give my son willingly back to

God, or do I hold onto him in my heart and become angry with God for taking my sweet baby?

If I was going to be used of God during this difficult time, I would have to willingly give Him my son. So I knelt. Once again I poured my broken heart out to God. I begged Him to help me to give my son to Him without any anger or bitterness in my heart. Without resentment or even begrudgingly, but rather willingly hand Elioenai over just as Hannah had done and so did Abraham in the Old Testament with his son.

Do you remember the story of Abraham and Isaac? God gave Abraham and Sarah a child in their old age. They had been promised a child and when Sarah was in her nineties, the Lord gave them Isaac. Their promised child brought incredible joy and they delighted in him as most parents do with their children. However, the Lord asked something of Abraham that was not expected and would certainly be challenging. He told Abraham to take his son and sacrifice him on an altar. Without question Abraham prepared to do just that. He gathered the materials needed and hiked up the mountain with his son. Isaac at one point asked his father where the offering was and Abraham's reply was, "God will provide".

Abraham trusted the Lord to provide a sacrifice, but even if that was not the Lord's plan he was still going to obey God. Abraham had already laid Isaac on the altar and with knife in hand raised and ready to sacrifice his son, the Lord called out and revealed the ram caught in the thicket. God asked something very difficult of Abraham. He asked for the life of his son. I would dare say the majority of us would gladly lay down our lives for our children. We would rather suffer pain than see our child suffer. Yet, that is not what God asked of Abraham, he did not ask that he sacrifice himself. He asked for Isaac to be sacrificed. The Lord is fully aware of how much a parent loves his child, and He wants at times to see if we are going to put that child before Him or if we will obey despite the difficult and seemingly impossible circumstances.

God requested a similar thing from my husband and me. He asked for the life of our son. God's plan for our son's life had already been fulfilled in those short eighteen weeks and He was ready to call our son home. So there I knelt and as I prayed, the Lord began to answer. He helped me to lay my son on the altar and say, "Here he is Lord, the life of my precious son whom I love so much. My little boy whom I have prayed over and only shared 18 weeks with. My son

that I miss deeply already, I give him back to You."
The Lord brought such a peace as I let go of my anger
towards God for taking my son from me, and that is
when the healing process could really begin.

Chapter Nine

Learning To Move Forward

My in-laws were able to fly out a week after everything happened. When we arrived back to the house and had put the kids to bed my, father in-law handed us a letter he had written to our sweet Elioenai boy. His thoughtfulness was touching, and we began to share with them a few more of the details of little Eli's birth. Everyone in the family dealt with grief in different ways. My husband and I grieved for our child and my mom and in-laws grieved for not just their grandchild, but also for their children. I cannot imagine how it must have felt to be in their shoes to see their grown son in such agonizing grief.

We had a wonderful week long visit with them and after they left to go back home, we were on our own for the first time since all of this happened. I began to slump with discouragement and even loneliness. I wanted to have my husband at home but he had to go back to work. Life did not stop just because our child had died. I had a hard time coming to grips with that. It did not seem right that everyone else had moved on with their lives and I did not know how to. The Lord sent just the encouragement I needed one day in the mail. A friend of ours sent us a letter with a very sweet gift. She and her husband had also lost a child a few years previously and in her words she said, "Though everyone else moves on, you will just feel stuck." How true!

I remember telling my husband, "I don't know how to move on from here and I don't know that I want to move on!" To me, moving on meant that I may forget about what happened and forget about little Eli. I did not want to forget it, any of it! Though most of the memories held such pain for me, they were the only memories of our sweet little boy that I would ever have! Though I knew he was in Heaven and was perfect and felt no pain, I did not want to hurt his feelings. I did not want him to feel left out and alone or that he could be so easily forgotten as if his life never mattered.

Oftentimes I would write letters to my sweet boy, explaining how I felt. On our son's three week birthday in Heaven I wrote him a letter and made it a blog entry.

Dear sweet boy of mine,

Happy 3 week birthday son! What a way to celebrate, in Heaven! I envy the angels right now, being able to spend all the time in the world with you. I have never lost someone whom I love like this. It is a hard journey for me, but I will do it, for you. I will carry you in my heart all the days of my life. When the Lord decides it is my time to join you, I must warn you, you should brace yourself. The big-gest hug I know how to give will be coming your way. I cannot wait to wrap my arms around you. I cannot wait to tell you every-thing I ever wanted you to know. I cannot wait to sing with you in praise to our God. I cannot wait to look in your eyes and see who you resemble. I cannot wait to see the color of your hair. I just can't wait.

At times it seems too long of a wait. At times the ache to hold you seems so great. The Lord never gives us something we cannot handle without Him. I wondered if maybe this was one of those situations, where it would be too difficult. However, the Lord has carried me through this journey. I have been far to weak to walk, my heart is still in pieces, my legs are to heavy to take the next step. The Lord has so graciously picked me up to keep me moving forward. Part of me doesn't want to move forward, I don't want you to ever be forgotten. I wish I could show you off to the world!

Three weeks ago today you made your entrance in this world. I remember the love for you that washed over me as I held your tiny frame. I wallowed in those all to few precious moments with you. We took your picture over and over just as we did for your brother and sister when they were born. I felt the same protectiveness over you when you were born. I made sure the nurses would treat you with respect, even though your life was gone from your body. Once a mommy always a mommy, no matter the case.

I have shed so many tears for you, son. Far to many for me to count, but the Lord has kept up with them. I am not angry with God for taking you so soon to be with Him. You are far too precious to be here on this earth. Though our weeping will endure for some time, I know that one day He will ease the ache. That doesn't mean we will miss you any less. You will forever be a part of our lives. You have taught us so much throughout all of this. Thank you, my sweet sweet boy.

I know you are perfect up there in Heaven, but just humor me. Be sure to say "yes sir", be sure to be polite and be friendly. Be sure to mind your manners, elbows off the table, chew with your mouth closed. No running in the halls, don't grow up to quickly. Don't forget your mommy and daddy. Remember, we love you SO much! Give everything you are to the Lord. Give the Lord a hug for me, extra tight and tell Him thank you for taking such good care of you in our stead.

On this your 3 week birthday in Heaven, though I wish you were still here with us, I wish you the happiest of birthdays. You, my son, I cannot wait to hold again! I love you.

Love,
Mommy

Every word I wrote was written with all the love a mother has for her child. Every word was written through blurred vision as tears pooled in my eyes. Each day seemed like a milestone. "Alright," I thought, "I made it through another day." With every day that passed, it was one more day away from the loss of our son; and time moved slowly by.

Yet, in the midst of all these passing weeks, the Lord was still so good to us. We heard back from the offer we had made on a house just before the loss of our son. Our offer was accepted, and we would begin to move forward in the closing process. Praise the Lord!! It was such a joyous time in the midst of such a trying time. I think it is no coincidence that the Lord allowed this wonderful event to take place, and the timing of it could not have been better.

You see, the Lord planted this trial right in the middle of two very wonderful events. The first event was what brought us out to Arizona in the first place. The Lord saw fit to place us in a new ministry and we loved the area where the Lord had just transplanted us, and we were beginning to build relationships with the members of our church. Then came the loss of our son, but it was closely followed by the accepting of our offer on our new home. God did not have to do that. He did not have to time it all so perfectly, but He did because He loves us immensely! In the midst of our valley He wanted us to know, "Hey, I'm still here, I still care, and I still love you!"

That is a truth about God I had known, but one that hit home even further because of this event. I have always *known* that God is with me at all times and that He constantly and consistently loves me, but in my darkest hours it meant even more to know that He was there with me still.

Now, even though I knew God was with me and I was comforted by that fact, there were times when my heart struggled over being angry at Him for allowing this to all take place. One night as Chad and I lay in bed, I began sharing with him my struggles for that day. I told him that as I mopped my kitchen floor, I wanted to get mad at God and have Him give me all of the answers as to why He allowed this to take place. I struggled with not having any answers. I struggled with maybe Chad finding me inadequate. Did he wish he had married someone else because my body, now for the second time, had been unable to carry our children to full term? Did he blame me for the heartache he had to go through?

None of these thoughts were planted in my head because of something he had said or done. It was just my mind running all different directions. Chad was more than quick to assure me all my thoughts were none of his. He was quick to assure me how much he loves me, and how much it hurt him to see me hurting so deeply. I do not deserve him but I am tremendously thankful for Him! I still felt a sense of guilt and responsibility for what happened. I felt like I could sense Satan wanting me to step over the line and become furious with God. The temptation was very real. Yes, even as a Pastor's wife, I struggled with being angry at God.

At times I did ask "why?" and through that time of questioning the Lord, I learned sometimes I have to be content when silence is God's answer for the present moment. Learning to be content is the key.

It is not easy to not have the answers laid out in front of. It is not easy to hear the doctor say, "We do not know why this happened; sometimes it just does". Learning to be content with no answers right when I wanted them is a lesson that I am still learning.

Through this difficult time of learning different lessons about God, I began putting pressure on myself to *get back to normal*. I felt like I should not be struggling so much once a few weeks had passed. Shouldn't I put on my happy face and jump back in the game of life?

If I am going to be completely honest, I must admit that I felt the same pressure from others also. I remember being pulled aside one evening after church was over and being completely blind-sided by the conversation. I had made my blog public with a desire to share how I was dealing with the loss of our son in an attempt to help other women who have been or were going through the same situation. In my writings, I was very honest about struggles and victories and always made a point to remind myself and my readers that God is good all the time. I truly wanted to give God glory through what He had done and was continuing to do. So the conversation that took place completely threw me off guard. The lady told me I needed to stop writing on this blog and take it down because many of the women in our church were reading it, and she did not feel it was good for them to know that the youth pastor's wife was struggling with God's plans for her life. Wait, what?

Now, I know this may shock some of you, but at the risk of increasing heart attacks, I am going to take the plunge and reveal a secret I have. Are you ready for this? Take a deep breath and breathe out slowly, here goes. I am human. Yes, I know a real shocker right? Let me give you a moment to let that sink in.......all right, have you recovered yet?

The truth is, though my husband and I are in the ministry, we are just like every other Christian who struggles in their Christian walk from time to time. You will find no "Super Christians" here in our house, just your average human being learning every step of the way how to grow and trust in Jesus more with every passing day. It is a joy to be in the ministry, but just like those who are not in ministry, we can struggle with similar issues and grief just takes time.

Ministry does not change our humanness simply because the role we play in church gives us a title of "Pastor's wife". Sometimes we struggle with having enough faith to get through the tough times.

Sometimes we struggle with daily devotions and sometimes we struggle through temper tantrums from our children. Is it beginning to sound like what goes on in your home? One wonderful thing about ministry is that God knows and sees all of this and has still chosen to use us humans to fulfill His work on earth. He uses ordinary people to accomplish great things for Him! Think about it, if God only used "super Christians" to accomplish what He wanted done, we would never be able to relate to them! What person can relate to a perfect Christian?

Remember Moses back in the Old Testament? Once he found out who he really was, an Israelite, he forsook the life he had once known. A life of promise, pampering, and ruling! It took faith to walk away from all of that. His faith did not stop there though. God wanted Moses to go before Pharaoh and request that God's people be freed. Do you remember Moses' response? Something along the lines of "You want me to do what? Why me? I can't even speak right! I have a stammering tongue!"

Yet what did God do? He reminded Moses He was well aware of how His tongue worked because He replied with, "Moses, I made your tongue!" God also used Moses to accomplish great things for Him!

When he stepped into the Red Sea and the waters divided for the Israelites to walk across, there was no super Christian leading the way. It was simply a man allowing God to work in His life. It is never the super Christian at work because there is no such thing. When great things are accomplished for God through someone, it is only because that person is allowing God to work through them. All of the glory belongs to Christ, and if we were perfect Christians we would take all of the glory for ourselves. That is just how our ugly sinful nature works.

During this time of heartache, I would repeat over and over to God, "Your will, not mine. Please, use this situation to bring glory to Yourself!" God proved during that time, just as He did with Moses, to be the great I AM. What exactly does it mean to be the great I AM? In simple terms it means that God is everything we need for that present situation. He is all we need.

No matter how rough the day was, God's grace was still overwhelmingly present. At times it seemed He was sitting right next to me with His arm around me. He knew that was what I needed. The Lord literally carried us through our valley. Am I angry at God? Am I wavering in my faith? Do I doubt His perfect will for our lives? No. Honestly, no. Though at times the temptation was there, I Corinthians 10:13 is a reality,

> *"There hath no temptation taken you but such as is common to man: but God is faithful, who will not suffer you to be tempted above that ye are able; but will with the temptation also make a way to escape, that ye may be able to bear it."*

Praise the Lord! The truth is, dear friend God is real. Faith is REAL. Christianity is a day in day out REAL relationship. Sometimes it is a struggle. Sometimes the days seem overwhelming. Sometimes the grief of life can weigh heavy on our hearts. BUT God is *ALWAYS* there. He is right in the midst of that storm holding onto us with His strong, capable loving hands. He is faithful and does not abandon His children in the midst of their heartbreak. He is good all the time, and all the time He is so good. Is this something that you believe in your heart of hearts?

God is completely worthy of our praise at all times. Whether the circumstances are great or simply downright difficult, keep in mind that our circumstances are not what determines how much or how little praise we should give God. He is an unchanging God. That means He is good all the time, all–the–time! He is worthy of our praise at all times. Just look at what the Psalmist David wrote in Psalm 34:1

"I will bless the LORD at all times: his praise shall continually be in my mouth."

Now I do not know about you, but I do not gather from the verse that it is a suggestion to praise the Lord. I do not read the Psalmist saying, "If you want to or if you feel like it praise the Lord." Nope! David had it right when he wrote it with quill and ink! Come on, Christian, bless the Lord always! Let His praise *continually* be in your mouth!!

Because I was curious, I looked up the definition of continually in Webster's Online Dictionary. Do you know what the very first definition was? Here it is and I quote:

"Seemingly without interruption"[2]

Sounds pretty self-explanatory to me. Now let's put this definition into practical every day use. When you are running late and the car battery is dead, praise the Lord. When the promotion you were certain to get but was handed over to someone younger

---

[2] "continually." webster-dictionary.org 2013 http://www.webster-dictionary.org/definition/continually (3 October 2014.

with not nearly the talents you have, praise the Lord. When God decides it is time to call your child or other loved one home to be with Him sooner than what you and I think is right, praise the Lord. Earnestly thank the Lord for what He is doing in your life even if you are not sure what He is doing. Even if you have no glimpse at what the future holds, have faith and trust that He knows what He is doing. Christ only has our best interest in mind, and He will be everything we need. What a comforting truth to cling to in our great times of need!

Chapter Ten

Healing Comes Only
Through Christ

everal years have now passed since the passing of our son. The Lord has helped to heal the wound in my heart, but I am not the same person I was before going through the loss of my son. Oh no, once a mother holds the lifeless body of her child, she is forever changed. The Lord has allowed my husband and I to lose a total of five babies now, and though no amount of children we ever have had or will have will ever replace the ones who are now awaiting our arrival in Heaven, the Lord has been gracious and gifted us with another baby girl to raise here on earth!

When we found out that our sweet baby girl was on the way, we were thrilled and I was honestly a bit apprehensive. I feared losing another baby, but wanted so much to rely on God's strength. I did not want to fear my entire pregnancy with her. I wanted to enjoy it, and the only way to do so was to place my fears of what could happen, into the all capable hands of my Jesus.

Finding out our expectant baby was a little girl, we began tossing names back and forth! That is always an adventure! We both loved the name Alyssa and when we discovered the meaning of the name, we knew it would be perfect for our little gift! Alyssa means "Joy, great happiness" and we went with the middle name of Joy, my middle name. We often refer to Alyssa as our "double joy" because that is just what she is! She has been constantly full of joy and smiles! She made her arrival the day after Christmas in 2012. What a sweet Christmas gift the Lord gave to us!

We know that trials are always going to be a part of our lives. Those trials will be difficult to go through, but we have also learned that no matter how dark the night may be, joy will come! The Lord will not abandon us. He will be our strength and see us through to the other side. As we face the refiner's fire, we can trust Christ and cling to His promise of faithfulness. Through Christ we have *hope*! There is hope for healing our broken and wounded hearts. Hope that we will one day see, face to face, the precious faces of our babies gone before us.

Dear friend, what are you struggling with today? What storm in life has you bound in fear? What trial is stealing your joy and hope in Christ, making it impossible to continue to praise Him? I challenge you; to turn your heart towards God. Though the temptation to turn from Him may be great, He really is the only One who can bring comfort and healing to your hurting heart. Keep in mind that though your situation may seem unbearable, He will never ask you, or make you, walk this path alone. He longs for us to let Him be our light to our path and carry our burdens for us. Kneel at the foot of the cross and ask Him for the faith you need to make it through the storms of life. Let's ask Him to teach us how to continue to praise Him through the storms.

Now, what if you are sitting there thinking, "I do not know Christ as my personal Savior"? What if you have never asked Christ to forgive you of your sins and asked Him to be your Savior? How can I cling to Christ through my pain when I do not even know

Who He is? Oh friend, may today be the day of your salvation! Romans 3:23 tells us:

> *"For all have sinned, and come short of the glory of God;"*

We all sin, we all mess up, and we all fall so short of God's glory. I John 1:9 gives clear instruction though,

> *"If we confess our sins, he is faithful and just to forgive us our sins, and to cleanse us from all unrighteousness."*

Here is the good news! There is *hope*, and Acts 16:31 says,

> *"Believe on the Lord Jesus Christ, and thou shalt be saved"*

All you have to do is believe on the name of the Lord Jesus Christ and He will save you! It is a promise! Realize that you are a sinner in need of a Savior and are on your way to hell. Ask the Lord to forgive you and to cleanse you from all your wicked sinfulness and ask Him to come and accept the free gift of salvation that He is offering to you. It is that simple, by grace alone through faith alone. Salvation is a gift waiting to be received. Why not accept it today?

Trials will come. They are a fact of life. They come in all shapes and sizes, and we never know when one will hit. The question is, what are we going to do about it when they do come? I encourage you; keep your eyes on Christ. Remember, it is alright to hurt; it is alright to grieve. These are normal human responses that the Lord Himself gave us. It is up to us though to make the choice to keep on praising Him through it all. Remember friend, God is good all the time, and all the time He is so good.

CPSIA information can be obtained
at www.ICGtesting.com
Printed in the USA
LVOW03s2038231117
557349LV00007B/185/P